Become The Person You Want To Be

With very best wishes

from

Wendy Thrippleton

written & designed by wendy thrippleton

First published in 2011 by:

Live It Publishing
27 Old Gloucester Road
London, United Kingdom.
WC1N 3AX
www.liveitpublishing.com

Printed by Print On Demand Worldwide, UK, USA & Australia.

All enquiries should be addressed to Live It Publishing.

ISBN 978-1-906954-38-3 (pbk)

Acknowledgements

This book is dedicated to my dear mum Rosemary Thrippleton who died 3 years ago. Also to my family Denise Pethick, Andrew Thrippleton, Sue Robinson, Sharon Thrippleton.

I could not have written this book without the ongoing support of my twin sister Sue Robinson who always said "get on and write this book", she has opened my whole life up.

Also a big thankyou to Heather and John Marytn for their endless love and support.

Many thanks to my friend Ben Crimp who has helped and encouraged me from the start.

Not forgetting all my dear friends, they have also been wonderful.

About The Author

Wendy Thrippleton is a self-employed card and canvas designer based in Totnes, S.Devon. She produces personalised digital images and artwork combining a variety of subjects including florals, pure abstracts, outdoor life, seascapes, landscapes, portait images. These images have made their own way onto greeting cards, postcards, canvases, and meditation cards.

How To Use This Book

This book contains powerful coloured images which take you on a magical journey with full guidance showing you great potential and a greater level of awareness. You will find the true you, which is so important in bringing influence of power.

This book is designed to strengthen your connection to receiving total guidance found within the coloured images and text, which will dissolve any forms of fear.

Turn these pages slowly listen to these words and see the coloured images bring freedom to awaken your heart.

Each page contains a powerful message to help you have a positive day.

Don't worry if you have a busy life, just pick out the words that you need to get you through the day. You can use this book anytime of day or night.

It's best to keep the book on a bedside table or counter, so you can refer to it whenever you need a boost to get you through a day.

Expand your growth as you go through life.

It's great fun being you.

Become The Person You Want To Be

There's no need for fear, as you can now live your life at your highest potential.

Don't let people hold you back, let the light of the flame burn only positive energy, and see yourself beginning a new journey which is connected to God's infinite light and wisdom.

Know you can now see your life becoming as it was originally planned.

You are free at last to attract all the good you deserve.

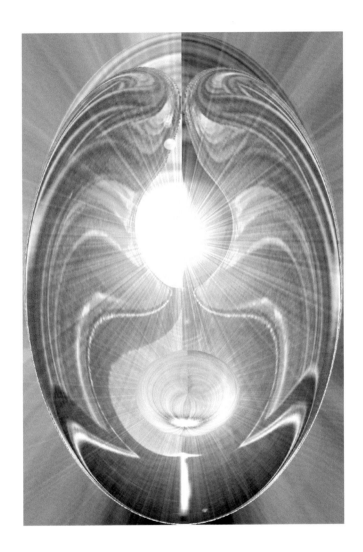

Diamond Of Wealth

See this diamond bring wealth to you.

Imagine things happening that will mirror your reflections, bringing wealth your way.

Everthing that you desire is yours.

You will meet all your earthly needs, you now have the knowledge.

Dreams Can Come True

Believe in your dreams - focus on the centre of the image.

Now unfold your dreams and see them ahead shining brightly with God's divine love.

Allow yourself to believe all your dreams will come true and they will.

Shine for who you are truly meant to be.

Live for today as time is so precious.

Never give up, you can be anything you want to be... Just believe!

Keep Centred

Be free knowing you are centred, focus in the centre of the image and concentrate - observe everlasting joy.

Be thrilled as you see your dreams become dynamic.

Observe your dreams.

There are no limitations as you have total control.

See all your dreams come true.

Galaxy Whirl

Centre yourself by looking at the middle of the image - this will ground you.

Increase your energies and see the light within.

Cherish yourself wholly and see your life as you have never seen it before.

Always believe, never give up for you can be anything you want to be.

Gate Of Abundance

Seek out the wonder that is in you, for your light is flawless.

See your shining light as dawn breaks pushing the dark clouds of the night right into the distance.

You now have found your keys to the gate of abundance.

Love life always, keep wisdom in your heart and really be the person you were meant to be.

God's Endless Love

Know the true you, as you are embraced in God's love.

Remember we are all in this bubble with God's endless love and protection.

Hold on to your dreams, as God will bring light upon you.

Shine like a star, as God makes you whole again.

He has made all the bridges you need, so you can cross any situation and do incredibly well.

Pour your love and light out to others.

There is no problem God can't solve. God puts his hands together and prays with you, he bows and applauds you well done!

Stay in his light, it never fades.

Be at one always.

Graphic Colours

Return and reappear with distinctive graphic colours, you are now making conception as many colours take your breath away.

Recoil reclaim your power, so be self-reliant, independant and in control.

Highest Potential

Take control of your life, as you have a level of self-awareness.

The Golden Wheel brings many opportunities.

Keep your eye on the center of the wheel and see your doorway open as you now have new awareness.

Trust what you receive, as you have endless guidance for your future.

See the light ahead for you now hold the key to your life and know you are never alone.

Walk ahead with pride always.

Know Your Way

See the light that is within you, for you know you have the strength within to be the person you want to be!

Your flame will light your heart alive, so you can know the way in life.

Live for your goals and feel them as they come alive.

May your heart and soul be full of your dreams.

Your power of light will always light up your true path.

Light Of The World

Let your light shine so people can see the real you.

You have been held back in the past but this is your time.

Dissolve your darkness so your light can shine out, as the light of your world.

See yourself come alive, never mind what people say just be yourself.

Point your light so you can clear your path, you are now free from the past.

Have no more fears, as your flame has dissolved your darkness.

Rekindle Your Candle Flame

Let your energy and light be cocooned and encased for your heart has a shell to keep it free from the harshness of today's life.

You can rekindle your candle flame and open your conscience and live the life of happiness, for nothing can break through the shell of your heart, as it has a strong beat that will never fade.

See The Path Ahead

Clear the space around you.

Take a few moments to centre yourself with some deep breaths.

Imagine yourself surrounded by a beautiful sparkling golden light.

Know that nothing can stand in your way.

There are no limits to what you can be.

Feel the energy from the beam of light, as it holds powerful rays of light.

Be prepared for big surprises, as this image holds love plus a strong force.

It has a beam of light that can be seen anywhere, it has no limits, so hold on to the powerful beam, as it will always bring light into any dark situation.

Stand firm and know who you truly are.

Take action and change many situations for the better.

Begin your true path to walk forward and see the path a head.

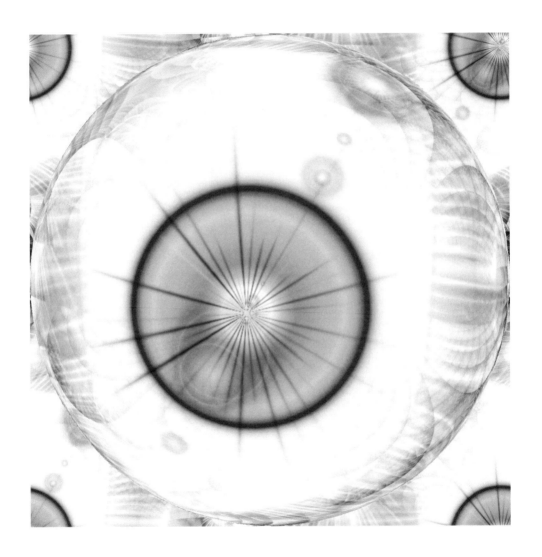

See Yourself For Who You Are

Drift away see yourself for who you are.

The journey ahead is a fabulous event, believe and see yourself over take the past, the under current has gone so you can stand up to the ultimate path of your life!

Feel the atmosphere as Angels of Heaven are hovering in flight to unclutter your mind, so it is only now you are unrestricted and set free.

The Empire is your Kingdom.

Shine For Who You Are

Shine your light out showing who you really are.

Don't hold back for you know you have the power of your flame shining out from the heart.

Don't doubt yourself for your power of light can be seen for many miles.

Shine your beacon, never let your light be extinguished out.

Nothing will ever dampen the glowing flame for today and evermore.

Star Of The Future

Celebrate the star of the future. You have forthcoming events approaching so capture this time, gather all you can, trust in yourself and be delighted when you look back just how well you have done.

The Light Of Love

Stand up and be aware as you have a big opportunity to walk forward and find the door way to your temple.

You will find purification and divine love when you look beyond the beam of light.

Step into the light daily, knowing you are now restored.

A great life awaits you, for the time is now offering you everything.

The Universe

Feel the emotions as you are truly inspired by your triumphs.

You have now cleared the path so you can now become the true you.

Transmit your messages to the universe.

Work with colour and feel the frequencies of colour and light.

See your goals appear and bring them to life for nothing can stop you now.

Your Magical Star

Begin your life for your star has appeared.

Make a new beginning, have a head start by embarking on your first step to activate your true life.

Discover the secrects behind the magical star.

Follow Your Path

See your life and catch sight of just how life can be.

Observe and witness the universe protect us from the forces of darkness.

Unleash yourself as you have been released free, let go and walk ahead and follow your true path, for the Angels have given you self confidence to know your direction in life!

Follow the light as you hold the torch of life.

Share the golden light with others, for they are golden roots that will never die.

Always see life in the eye of the light.

Believe And Have Faith

Stand back be firm and know you can unlock your heart to a brighter life.

Push all your worry away, you have the key that will open your heart.

Honour value your innerself, as this is so benefical.

A force is within so you have the strength and power to pull yourself through the key hole to be free from trouble, believe and have faith and know it's true, as you are now through the key hole.

Be free always.

Love Heart

Cherish those around you, see people for who they are, extend and deepen your love.

Let the streams of light overflow abundant love.

May all living beings find the opportunity to dissolve their problems into light, transforming us to a place of merit, for this is ever lasting happiness and joy.

You now have a new life be sincere, feel the force of opportunity and the strength of courage.

You can do anything.

Fly Away

Take flight and slip away, escape from the troubled world, as you now realize you can focus on your life.

Proceed as you are guided right through life.

Appreciate your life as you have a great outlook.

You are very successful, and there are many good things approaching.

Feel the abundance of love and life, remember you can always take flight and pass life with flying colours.

Be dynamic today.

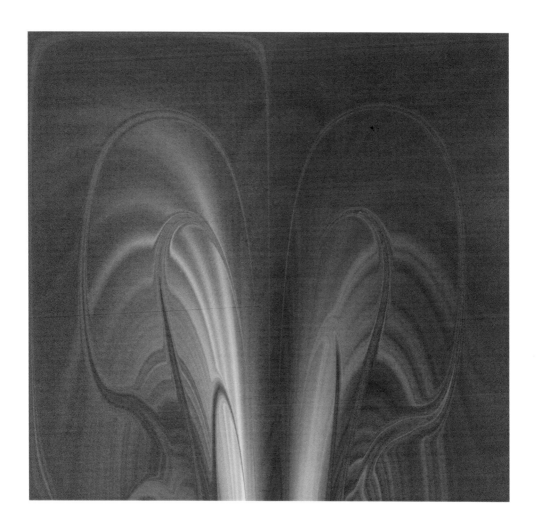

Stand Firm

Stand firm and know you have divine protection.

Do not worry as you know the true way!

Observe and submit to the Lord's divine protection as he sends direct guidance.

Believe you remain in God's endless love, for the Lord is our true creator.

Proceed composed knowing you are level headed.

See true balance as you now have peace of mind, victory on all sides.

Strength is always with you when you turn to the foot of the cross.

True Path

Access your doorway, you now have permission to enter your true path as you know you are surrounded by love.

Visualise and predict what you inwardly know, enter the essence of true life.

Illustrate your life and be enthusiastic, go ahead for you now have the power to do anything you want.

Lead the way.

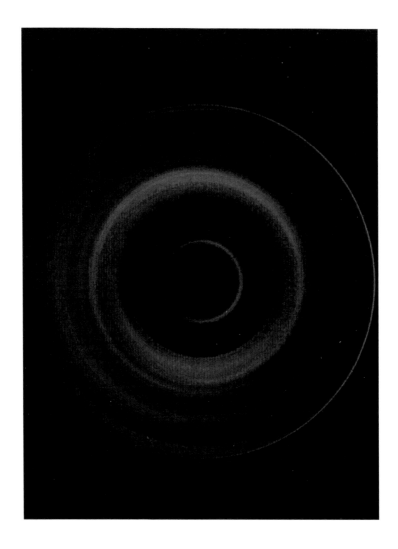

Self Assurance

Capture your inner self, for you have true command that gives you protected assurance.

Go about your day with security, which will make you calm and collected.

Be composed to bring full abundance and success to all you do.

Transmitting Strength

Hold on to the beauty within the image, engaging with the colours of love.

Cherish those around you, feeling their love and tenderness.

Believe in love and you will glow sending out the biggest beam of colours within your heart, so what ever happens in life you will be able to smile once again transmiting only a tower of strength, as this can't ever fall down.

Hold on to your strength.

Free And Energised

See the world as you wish to see it.

You can now make the right decisions, as you are given divine inspiration.

Believe in yourself, you can do anything, trust in your good judgement, feel energised and happy.

Escape To Victory

Here you are, escape from the troubled world.

Focus on success, understand and appreciate just how well you have done!

You are approaching victory, as you now have peace of mind.

True balance awaits you, abide with the realisation all will be well.

The power you have within is breathtaking.

Courage For Any Situation

Stand firm in the candle light flame, knowing at all times you have complete knowledge.

Recognize your true self now you have all the ability to knock down any negative thoughts.

You have been set free explore resemble and demand you will never get fearful as you have the courage to tackle any situation.

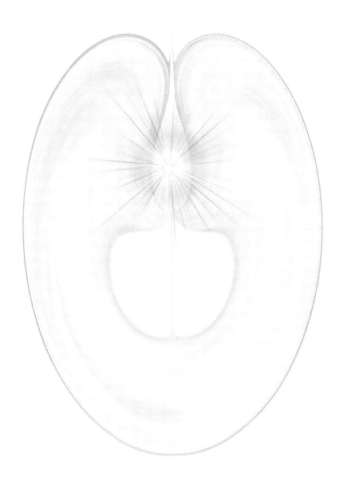

Bring Colour Into Your Life

Think of a wave carrying the energy of colour into your life.

Take your first step into the wave as it runs with you.

Make use of this wave as it makes you so strong the more times you ride the wave.

You have the natural ability to find the right course of action.

You now have the supreme power to be free from uncertainty or doubt.

Take part in the surfing on the crest of a wave.

Become outstanding in many ways.

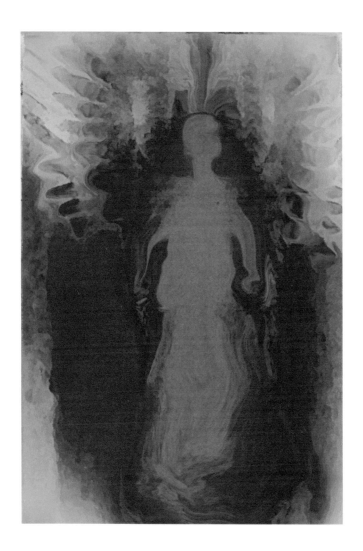

Harmony With The Universe

Be in harmony with the universe, look beyond what other people see.

Catch your breath and follow your dreams, generate love in abundance as you go on the journey.

Your universe will watch over you to protect you, gaze watch the sky and see the wonder of light that will guide and escort you back so you can now proceed with life, but now be a stronger person for your journey has been so beneficial, as you will know the direction of your dreams.

Angel's Shield

Transform your life as you wear this Angel Sheild.

The Angels will show you how to soar above all limitations.

Calm any worries as you regain a peaceful mind.

Trust your wisdom, and enjoy being your true self.

Take yourself to the depth and wonder of now entering a state of serenity and grace.

Wear this sheild with true pride, and honour your self-worth for life is full of many treasures.

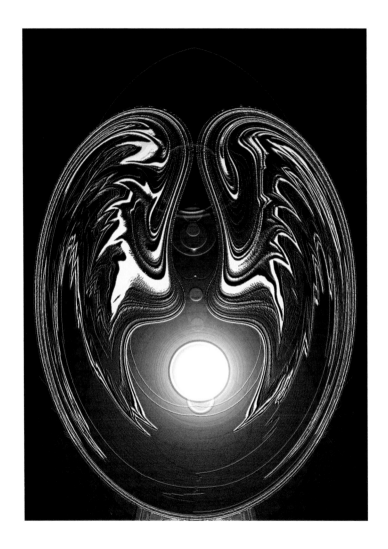

Spiritual Progress

Break through hidden fears and jump start your spiritual progress and experience an abiding sense of peace.

Become positive succesful and strong, as you respond to your inner needs.

Free yourself and explore the true you.

Obtain command as you know you are protected with divine love, so you reappear composed and very level-headed with peace of mind, with true balance and a strong victory on all sides.

Your outlook is very successful.

Enjoy!

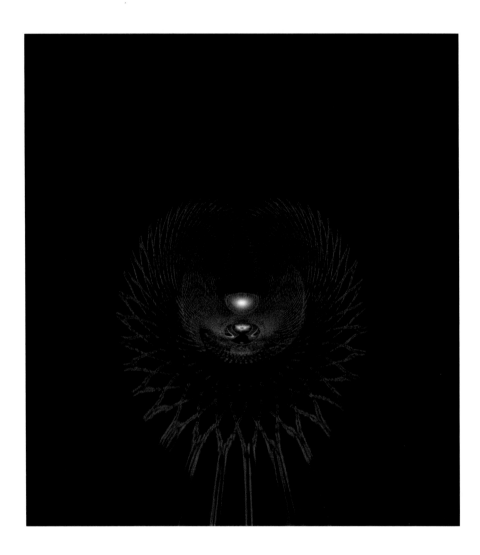

Shine Like The Golden Universe

Do not hide, shine like the golden universe as the light is within you.

We all have the choice to get through difficult times.

The great thing is whatever position you're in, you can always choose your very own path, the one that is your true path meaning the right path.

You are in a great position as you have full control to make your life work, take charge of your life.

You are all you have ever wanted to be.

All you ever need is there inside you, never doubt yourself because you know best.

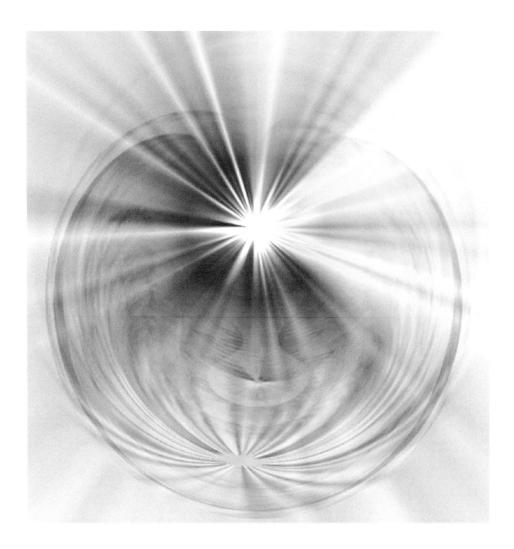

Mystical Teachings

Go through the black hole and feel the energy as you take yourself on a meditation.

See mystical teachings as your life comes together.

Understand your sole purpose right here, right now.

Discover the true joy of being yourself.

Be aware of the power of your subconscious.

See the light that is hidden within you - life will always be a brighter place.

There are no limits to what you can do!

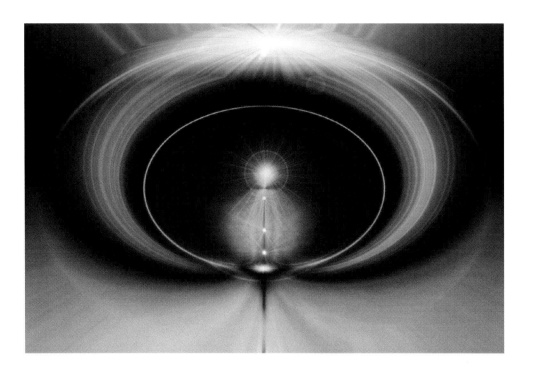

Seed Of Life

Take control and form your seed of life.

This is a new beginning you have true guidance, it's your turn to deliver as you have been rescued.

You have the ability to do anything you want.

Follow your heart and you'll get there for you have appeared.

Enjoy being the newcomer, because you are through the entrance.

You are here to stay.

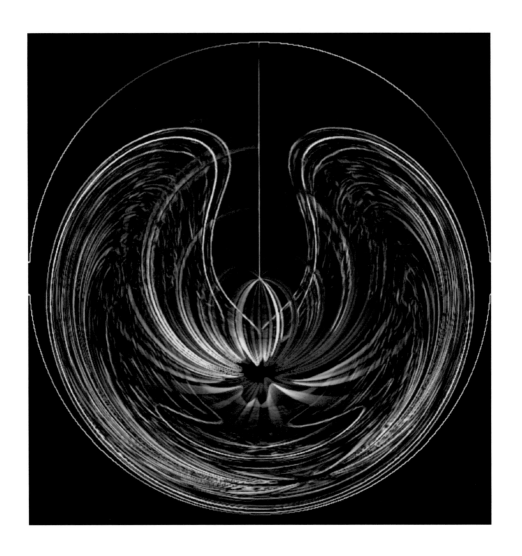

Connect To The Real You

Be amazed and connect to the real you.

Relax and reflect on all the good things.

Recharge your batteries because there are great things ahead.

Tap into the power of this energy boosting lantern and see that dreams do come true with long-term success.

Transmit Assurance

You are now brought back to full waking consciousness.

The important thing right now is visualise what you want, by seeing your dreams flow through your head, creating your personal choices and sustaining your mission in life.

Challenge your future growth, as your beacon of light will never blow out.

See your beacon light, know you have true assurance for you have the will power to make a big difference in today's world.

Inner Wisdom

Find your inner wisdom.

Change your focus on life, have the best year of your life.

Be in charge of your destiny.

Be passionate about bringing peace and harmony into your life.

Make a real connection today revealing your true magical spiritual self.

As the element of colour uncovers your hidden depths, release your past and see your future.

It's big - just open your eyes and see for yourself.

The End Goal

This book can really change your whole life.

Now you have read this book it can help you to understand the forces that control your life.

You can be in total control, walk through any door knowing you are in control, as you have the tools for any situation, you are in a great position.

Welcome the magic power - see your paths of destiny take control of your life.

Trust in yourself and have the wisdom of understanding.

Be at peace, I wish you well.

Attention Writers

Get published!

Everyone has a book inside of them. If you have the passion and determination to get it out there and tell the world, we can help you.

LIP works with new and established authors in the fields of:

- Personal Development, Self-Help, Popular Psychology & NLP
- Health, Healing & Alternative Therapies
- Motivational, Inspirational & Spiritual
- Business, Management & Entrepreneurship

We want to help you turn your creative work into reality!

Our innovative and progressive multi-media partnership publishing house will help you live the dream by getting your books, e-books, CDs and MP3s professionally published and distributed across a global network.

For more information visit our website at:

www.**liveitpublishing**.com

LIP... The easiest way to get published!